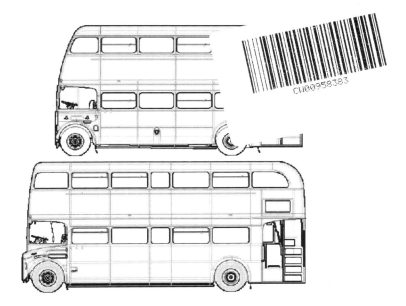

London Country's
Double Deckers

by Paul McKenzie

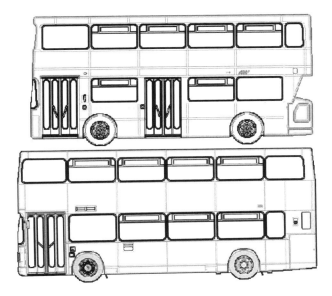

Contents

Introduction

This books concentrates on the double deckers buses in service with London Country from it's beginning on the 1st January 1970 until it was split into separate units ready for privatisation in 1986.

We start with the rear platformed vehicles acquired from London Transport such as the RT and Routemaster (both bus and coach form) and move on to the vehicles used to replace them, upgrade the fleet and convert to one man operation such as the Daimler Fleetline, Leyland Atlantean, Bristol VR and Leyland Olympian.

This book doesn't go into too much technical detail about each vehicle but is an overview of each type mainly to accompany my technical type drawings.

AEC Regent (RT)

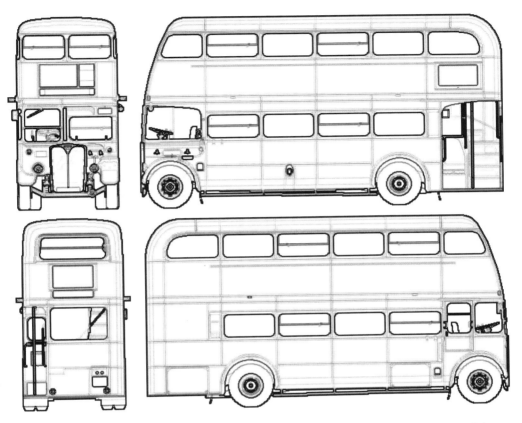

Upon it's beginning London Country inherited a number of RT's from London Transport and they initially carried on the routes as before, however London Country knew that crew operation wasn't ideal for the leafy suburbs and was looking to convert to one man operation as soon as possible. The first casualty's of this were the RT and by 1977 only a small handful remained. With some still needed on the 403 RT604, RT1018 and RT3461 even made it to being painted in to NBC green livery.

This didn't last long and by 1978 the final three had been withdrawn. Some of the earlier previously withdrawn ones were lucky enough to be sold back to London Transport and see out their final days there.

AEC Routemaster (RML)

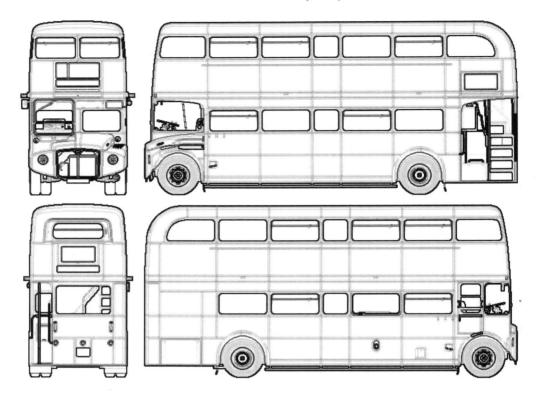

On 1st January 1970 London Country acquired 97 of the longer RML Routemasters during the split of the red and green areas. There was 100 originally but 3 had already been repainted red and returned to the City.

These carried on as they were, moving around to wherever needed but by 1977 the arrivals of Leyland Atlanteans and Leyland Nationals led to 29 being sold back to London Transport.

By 1979 withdrawals were increasingly taking place as LC become more one man operated and by early 1980 the final had been withdrawn and apart from two that were unfortunately scrapped they returned to see further service with London Transport.

Overall a great vehicle but much more suited to the city streets than the leafy suburbs.

AEC Routemaster Coach (RMC4)

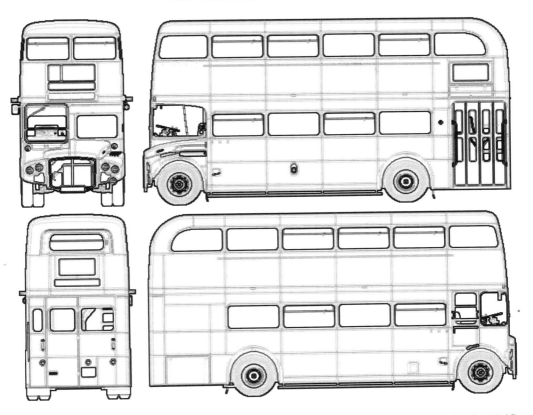

RMC4 started life as CRL4. It was the 4th Routemaster built and served as a prototype for the RMC class. Before passing to London Country during an overhaul it was made more like the RMC's and became renumbered to RMC4 but was still identifiable by it's different front destination display and it's nearside fuel filler cap.

When taken over by London Country it was already demoted to Bus duties and operated from Hatfield but it did well to last on these until 1979. It's special significance was then noted and it was retained for special duties and painted back into it's original Greenline colours.

AEC Routemaster Coach (RMC)

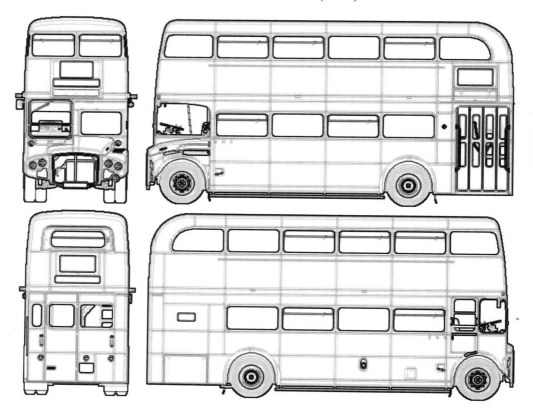

As well as RMC4 London Country inherited RMC1453-1520 which were still being used on Greenline services.

In 1972 with RP coaches arriving displacing the newer the RCL's the RMC's started to be demoted to standard bus work but I am sure the passengers welcomed this with their extra padded and more comfortable seating.

They continued on bus work until 1977 by which time the mass arrival of Leyland Atlanteans and Nationals led to them being withdrawn and all being sold back to London Transport who mainly used them as driver trainers.

AEC Routemaster Coach (RCL)

As well as the RMC's London Country inherited the longer RCL class of RCL2218-2260. Although being longer and slightly newer than the RMC's their history with London Country was very similar.

The first few started to be demoted to bus work during 1972 by RP's and then the great mistake started or replacing them on Greenline work with PVC bus seated LNC Leyland Nationals. However the RCL's settled down well onto bus work for a few years and like the RMC's they were withdrawn in 1977 and sold back to London Transport, most of them seeing further bus work there before moving on to the sightseeing fleet.

Daimler Fleetline (AF)

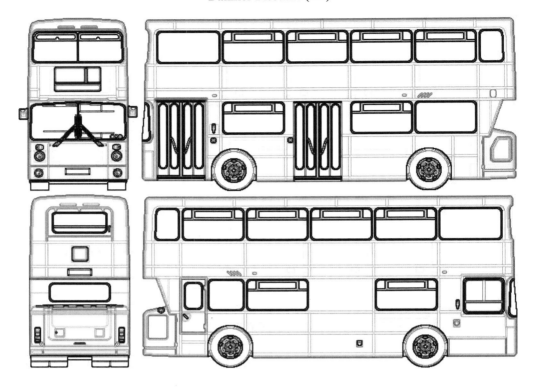

AF1-11   JPK101-11K

AF1-11 were London Country's first new double deckers arriving in January 1972. They were a diverted order from Western Welsh and LC snapped them up as they desperately wanted to start converting to OMO. They were used to replace RML's on route 410.

They only lasted 10 years with LC, being withdrawn by 1982 as they were non standard in comparison to the much larger AN class of Atlanteans.

With fleetnumbers and registrations only being 1 letter out from AN's 1-11 as well as being very visually similar you have to wonder if there was ever any confusion. The main difference between the Fleetlines and the Atlanteans was the AF's had a much simpler and plainer look to the front under the windscreen.

Daimler Fleetline (DMS)

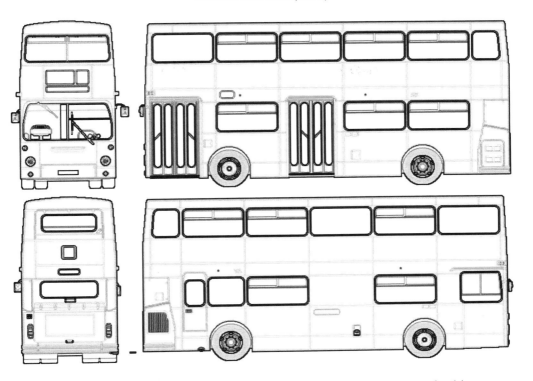

Further Fleetlines arrived in 1980 in the shape of 8 DMS's from London Transport for driver training purposes. At this time London Country didn't have any OMO double deckers available for training as they were all still in passenger service.

Leyland Atlantean (AN1-90)

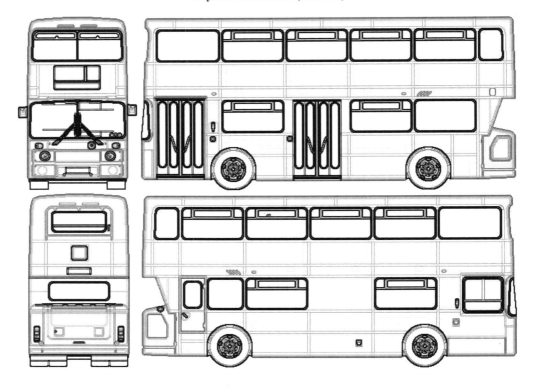

AN1-90   JPL101-90K

London Country's put in a large order for 90 Leyland Atlanteans to start improving the fleet and they started arriving in March 1972. These were bodied by Park Royal with two doors and a central staircase.

With such a large batch these were scattered far and wide over the system and proved to be a good and reasonably reliable vehicle for London Country. They did have some teething problems but nothing in comparison to the problems London Transport were having with their Fleetlines.

Leyland Atlantean (AN91-120)

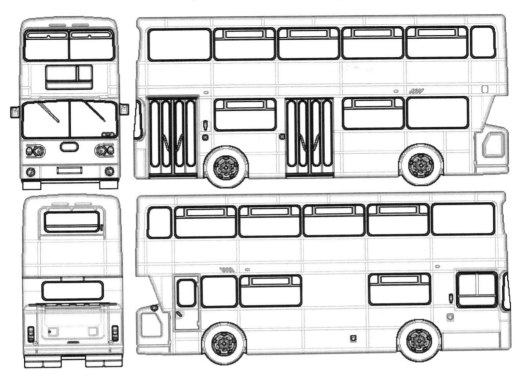

AN91-120   MPJ191-220L

In October 1972 NBC diverted a batch of 30 MCW bodied Atlanteans ordered for Midland Red to London Country where they were more desperately needed.

Despite being MCW bodied they were very similar to the Park Royals ones before, main differences being a different front lower panel, windscreen wipers at the top of the windows, no rear route number and the registration plate was now below the top deck above the lower deck window.

Leyland Atlantean (AN121-123)

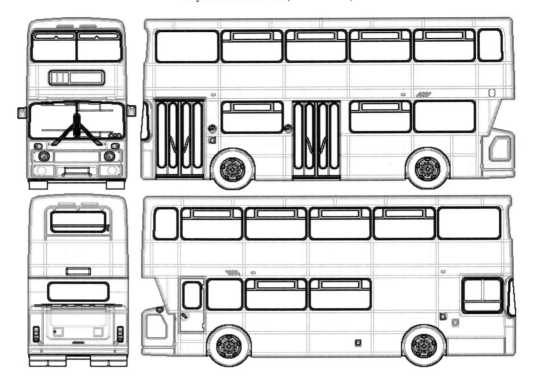

AN121-123   VPB121-3M

In 1974 a further three Park Royal Atlanteans arrived. These had quite a numerous amount of differences from the first 90. They still has two doors but the staircase had been moved forward to behind the driver rather than in the middle. Gone was the rear destination screen, gone was the wind screen wash cap on the front, they had a 3 track number and destination blind and the side indicators were now much smaller compared to the previous long tall ones.

It's worth noting that AN121 still survives to this day and is preserved in London Country North East livery.

Leyland Atlantean (AN124-237)

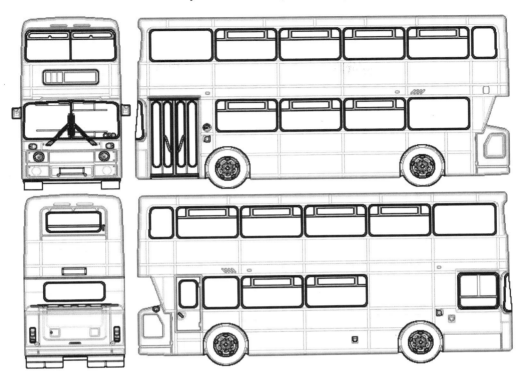

AN124-147   UPK124-47S
AN148-158   VPA148-58S
AN159-202   XPG159-202T
AN203-232   EPH203-32V
AN233-237   JPE233-237V

There was a few years gap but in 1978 the first of the Standard Atlanteans started arriving, I call them standard as they were the standard for the next few years with so many arriving and effectively standardising the London Country fleet.

AN124-183 were bodied by Park Royal and AN184 onwards by Roe although they were effectively exactly the same. There was only really one change since AN121-123 but it was very noticable in there was now no need for centre exit doors.

Leyland Atlantean (AN238-293)

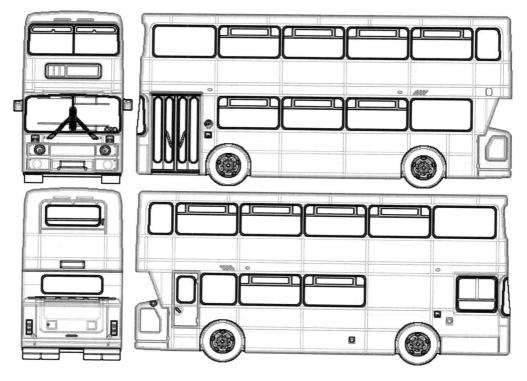

AN238-292   KPJ238-92W
AN293   MPJ293W

AN238 onwards were effectively exactly the same as the previous batch except they now had updated more square indicator side and front lights, the rear lights were also updated with a more square design.

AN293 was an add on to the order to replace AN99 that had been destroyed in a fire. This was the final new Atlantean to be purchased by London Country and spent it's entire life at Stevenage until sold to Yorkshire Rider.

Leyland Atlantean (AN294-305)

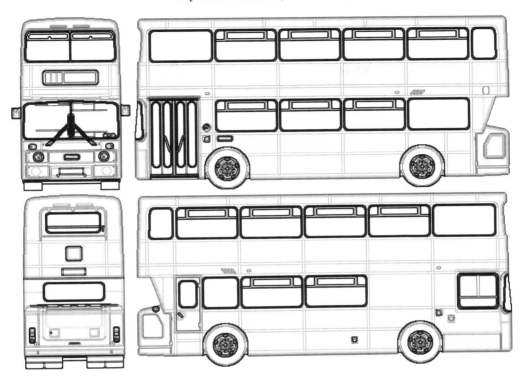

Chelsham garage desperately needed some more but cheap double deckers in 1985 for London Regional Transport services and they came in the shape of 12 from Southdown. These were Park Royal bodied so very similar to London Country's own examples, the main noticeable difference was the addition of a pay as you enter light on the front panel and another by the entrance door.

Leyland Atlantean (AN306-337)

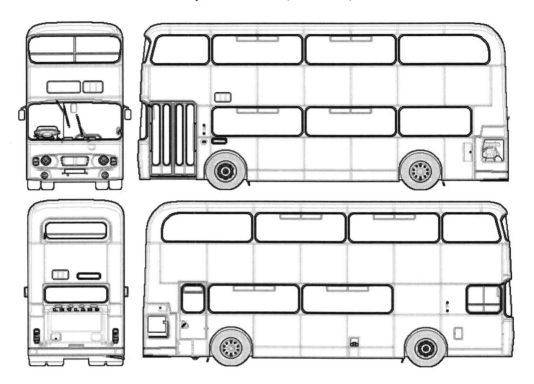

The need for further cheap double deckers resulted in a further 30 arriving from Strathclyde. These were very different beasts indeed with having Alexander bodies. Unusual features were the large panoramic windows (which actually led structural weakness) and the fact the windows didn't all line up. They were fine on the near side but the offside downstairs ones were set further back.

Further second hand Atlanteans did arrive once the companies had been split up bringing even more variety.

Bristol VR (BT)

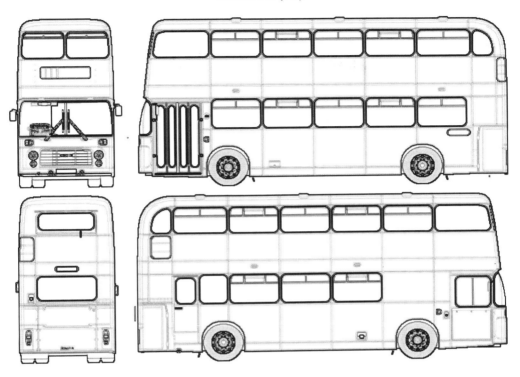

BT1-15   PPH461-75R

An unusual purchase in 1977 was of 15 Eastern Coach Work bodied Bristol VR's. Unusual in that London Country seemed to be standardising on the Atlantean at this time and also because they were full height examples, with most VR's and the body being designed for low height it made them look over tall.

They were used on the 370 between Grays and Romford. However they only lasted until 1980 when the opportunity arose to sell them on early to Bristol Omnibus.

Leyland Olympian (LR1-30)

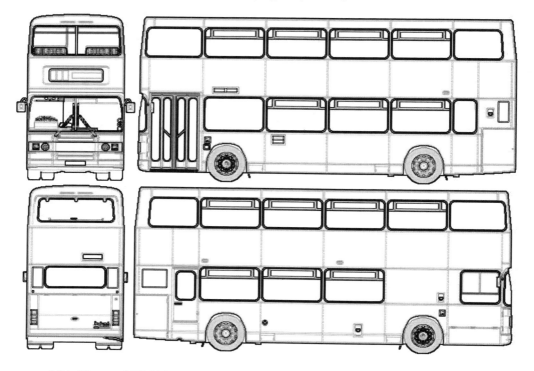

LR1-30   TPD101-30X

From 1982 the Leyland Olympian became the standard new double decker for London Country. This was Leyland's new double decker to using what they had learnt from the Atlantean, Bristol VR and Titan. They carried 72 seat Roe bodies.

Most of the first examples were used on newly won London Transport contracts.

Leyland Olympian (LR31-60)

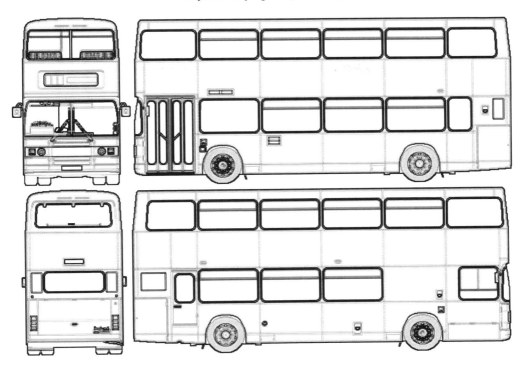

LR31-37	BPF131-7Y
LR38-45	A138-45DPE
LR46-60	A146-60FPG

The next batch of 15 had slight differences from the first 30, that being they now had fully opening side windows instead of partial ones and the rear number plate was now central rather than offset to the right.

Leyland Olympian (LR61-75)

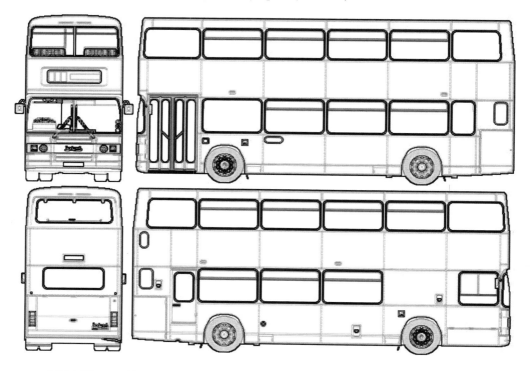

LR61-75   B261-75LPH

LR61 onwards were bodied by Eastern Coach Works rather than Roe but to the same design. A few differences that made these stand out were the Leyland scroll badge on the front grill, side indicators being moved to the rear of the wheel arch and the side grills being slightly different and more rounded, plus there was no longer any grills at the rear to the side of the lower deck window.

Early casualty's in this batch were LR63 which was written off during a head on accident with AN312 outside Hatfield garage and a few years later LR67 was destroyed by fire.

All the Olympians settled in well and provided good service to London Country and it's successors.

Leyland Olympian Coach (LRC)

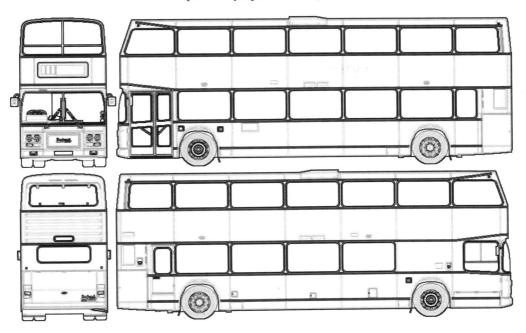

LRC1-5	A101-5FPL
LRC6-10	B106-110LPH
LRC11-15	C211-5UPD

The final double deckers purchased by London Country were 15 Eastern Coach Work coach bodied Leyland Olympians for use on Greenline work. The first were used on Kent commuter services and the later went on the Flightline 757 service linking Luton Airport to London with the final few being at Harlow for the 711.

Further Reading

Thank you for purchasing and reading my book and looking at my illustrations, if you enjoyed then please keep a look out for more additions in the series.

Other Books available in this series:
London Country's Leyland Nationals

Kind regards

Paul McKenzie

Printed in Great Britain
by Amazon